W9-BTE-567

The Wonder Series

OWLS

On Silent Wings

Written by

Ann C. Cooper

Illustrated by

Randi Eyre

and

Marjorie C. Leggitt

Denver Museum of Natural History
and Roberts Rinehart Publishers

DUCATION
ibRARY
UEEN'S UNIVERSITY
T KINGSTON
NGSTON ONTARIO CANADA

JU
QL696 .S83 C66 1994t

Text copyright © 1994 Ann C. Cooper

Artwork copyright © 1994 Denver Museum
of Natural History

All rights reserved

Published in the United States of America by
Roberts Rinehart Publishers
Post Office Box 666
Niwot, Colorado 80544

Published in Great Britain, Ireland, and Europe by
Roberts Rinehart Publishers
Main Street, Schull, West Cork
Republic of Ireland

Distributed in the United States and Canada by
Publishers Group West

Library of Congress Catalog Card Number 94-65092
International Standard Book Number 1-879373-78-5

Manufactured in the United States of America

Cover illustration derived from a photograph by Wendy
Shattil and Bob Rozinski

Page 4, pottery figurine by Nellie Bica, 1963,
Zuni Pueblo, New Mexico. Denver Museum of Natural
History, Crane American Indian Collection AC.6382

Page 4, from *Winnie-the-Pooh*, © E. P. Dutton, used by
permission of Dutton Children's Books, a division of
Penguin Books USA Inc.

Page 25, owl-eyed butterfly from Central and
South America, Zoology Department, Denver Museum
of Natural History

Page 63, pottery figurine, ca. 1950, Zuni Pueblo,
New Mexico. Denver Museum of Natural History, Crane
American Indian Collection AC.2394

Author Acknowledgements
–Danielle and Joshua Smith for allowing me to include
your story;
–Norman Smith for providing photographs from which
the illustrations for "Giving a Hoot for Owls" were drawn;
–Roberta Mantione and students at University Hill
Elementary School, Boulder, Colorado; and Beth Crosby
at Diplomat Elementary School, Cape Coral, Florida, for
sharing owl news from their schools.

Contents

Introducing Owls

Zuni pottery figurine

"And if anyone knows anything about anything," said Bear to himself, "it's Owl who knows something about something," he said, "or my name's not Winnie-the-Pooh."

A. A. Milne, *Winnie-the-Pooh*

All the animals in the story of Winnie-the-Pooh believe Owl is wise. They go to Owl for advice – including advice on how to find Eeyore's tail. You may wonder how wise Owl really is. He is using poor Eeyore's tail for a bell-pull! The tail hangs at the front door of Owl's treetop house and he doesn't even know it.

Perhaps owls are popular in stories because they look like small humans! Owls stand upright. Their slanting beaks look almost like human noses. Owls stare with huge, unblinking eyes. They may appear wise or studious. The truth is, owls are no more or no less wise than any other birds. They are just skillful hunters with special tools, including amazing eyes.

Whoo-whoo-whoo

Most owls hunt at night. The way they skim meadows or swoop through forests on silent wings adds to their aura of mystery. Often, the only clue of an owl's presence is a spine-chilling shriek or a ghostly *whoo-whoo-whoo*. Because of these cries in the dark, people used to think owls were evil omens. Did owls bring bad news or foretell death? Some people thought so. The truth is, owls call to communicate with other owls. They do not bring news of any kind to people – except the good news that an owl lives in the neighborhood!

How Horned Owl Found a Wife

As birds of the night, owls have often been associated with monsters, witches, and the coming of death in many Native cultures of North America. But the role of the owl is more complex among the Wabanaki, the Native people of northeastern America. Although sometimes the call of an owl might be an omen of ill fortune, owls were not always seen as bearers of bad tidings. The screech owl, Titgeli, often nested close to the edge of Wabanaki villages, giving a distinctive call when someone disturbed it late at night. In traditional lore, this owl was known as the village guardian – one who gives warning against dangerous intruders. When hunting, men often wore a cape with two ears on it to mimic the appearance of Kokohas, the horned owl. Disguised, they could creep close to the deer or the caribou.

The following story of an owl who falls in love with a young woman comes from the traditions of the Penobscot Indians, one of the Wabanaki nations of Maine.

ong ago, Horned Owl lived in a great pine tree with his old aunt. He was lonely and went looking for a wife. He flew from village to village, looking for just the right person to marry. At last he came to a Penobscot village by the side of a river. As he sat in a tree by the river, a young woman came to get water. As soon as Horned Owl saw her, he knew he wanted her to be his wife.

This young woman, though, was very proud of herself. Her name was Flowing Stream and she thought there was no man in the whole world good enough to marry her. Her parents reminded her that since she was grown she might think of taking a husband, but none of the young men in the village pleased her.

"That one is too fat," she would say, or "That one is too tall," or "I do not like the way he wears his leggings."

Finally, her father could stand it no longer.

"Daughter," he said, "tell us what it is that you want."

The daughter thought for a bit and then decided to ask for something that no one could do. That way she would be left alone.

"I will marry the first man who can spit into the fire and make it burn hotter."

Horned Owl heard all that from his perch in a cedar tree. He flew home to his old aunt.

"My aunt," he said, "I have found the one I want to marry, but she says she will not marry anyone unless they can spit in the fire and make it hotter."

Horned Owl's aunt scraped some of the resin from the bark of the pine tree.

"Put this in your mouth," she said. "Spit this onto the fire and it will burn hotter."

Horned Owl flew back to the edge of the village, where he turned himself into handsome young man. His two large tufts of feathers, however, still stuck up on his head. To cover them, he put on a two-eared cap.

Many young men had tried to make the fire burn brighter by spitting into it, but all had failed. Then Horned Owl strode into the village. Everyone was impressed by the tall young man.

"I have heard that your daughter will marry a man who can make the fire burn hotter by spitting into it," he said to Flowing Stream's parents.

"That is true," they said.

"Then I will marry her," Horned Owl said. He walked to the fire and spat out some of the pitch he held in his mouth. Immediately the flames flared up brightly.

Flowing Stream, though, was suspicious.

"Take off your cap," she said. "Let me see what you look like."

At first Horned Owl refused, but soon everyone in the village insisted. As soon as he took off his cap, his two feathered ears could be seen.

"I said I would marry the first man who could do what I asked," Flowing Stream said. "But this is not a man!"

Horned Owl was so embarrassed, he turned back into his own shape and flew quickly into the woods.

Now Flowing Stream decided that she did finally have to marry someone. But she wanted that person to be one who could care for her and her parents. "I will marry the man who brings in the most game by tomorrow night," she said.

Horned Owl, who was sitting again in the tree at the edge of the village, heard what she said. He was a great hunter and he hunted all that night and into the next day. Then he changed himself into the shape of a young man again, but this time one with very long, thick hair. He combed his long hair over his feathered ears and came into the village with all the game he had caught.

Everyone was impressed. This young man brought in twice as much as any of the others. Surely he should marry Flowing Stream.

Flowing Stream, though, was suspicious again.

"This young man looks familiar," she thought. Then she called him over to her. "Come and sit by the fire with me," she said.

Horned Owl sat down next to Flowing Stream. The fire was very hot and soon he began to sweat.

"Push back your hair from your face," Flowing Stream said. "Then you will feel cool."

As soon as Horned Owl pushed his hair back, his two feathered ears sprang up again.

"Look," Flowing Stream said. "This is not a man at all. It is the same one who tried to trick us before."

Once again, Horned Owl flew off disappointed.

Now Horned Owl was very sad. He sat in the tree near the edge of the village and began to sing a lonesome song. He sang about what a fine young woman Flowing Stream was and how much he wanted to be with her. He sang about how sad he was to always be alone.

In her wigwam, Flowing Stream heard Horned Owl's lonesome song and it touched her heart. What did it matter that he was different? He truly cared for her. She walked out into the forest and called to him.

"Horned Owl," she said, "I will marry you."

Then Horned Owl flew down to her and they were married. Horned Owl hunted for her and her parents and was a good husband. They were still living together happily when I left them.

Story by Joseph Bruchac

Who – Who's Who

Nearly 150 **species** (kinds) of owls live worldwide. They live everywhere except Antarctica and a few remote islands. Owls live in all kinds of **habitats** (living spaces), from arctic tundra to tropical rainforest, from old growth forests to deserts.

Some owls are widespread. Common barn owls are "everywhere" owls. They live in North America, South America, Africa, Europe, south and east Asia, and Australia. Common barn owls may live in towns, cities, farmland, prairies, marshes, and deserts.

Some owls live in just a few places in the world. For example, Seychelles owls live only on the Seychelles Islands in the Indian Ocean.

Other owls live in special and unusual habitats. Elf owls, for example, live in areas where giant saguaro cactus plants grow.

Wherever you live, at least three kinds of owls probably live nearby!

Activity: Owl Cards

Meet the 19 species of owls that live in North America.

Objectives: Use the cards to find which owls live in your area. As you read the book, refer to the pictures and facts on your "Owl Cards" when a new owl is introduced.

The game includes: "Owl Cards" on pages 11 and 13, and "Origami Owl" on page 44, to hold your cards when you are not using them.

You need: scissors

To play: Cut along the dashed lines to remove pages 11 and 13 from your book. Cut each page along the dotted lines to make "Owl Cards."

Who's Big, Who's Small ?

Some people think that all small owls must be babies. Not true! Owls come in many sizes. Least pygmy owls and elf owls are no larger than house sparrows, even when fully grown.

Great horned owls and snowy owls are larger than roosters. These owls stand about 2 feet (60 cm) tall. They have wing spans wider than your arms can reach (as wide as 5 feet [1.5 m]). By six weeks old, the **owlets** (baby owls) are as big as adults. They still look fuzzy and babyish at that age.

Large: (A) Great gray owl, (B) Great horned owl, (C) Snowy owl, (D) Spotted owl, (E) Barred owl
Medium: (F) Northern hawk owl, (G) Barn owl, (H) Long-eared owl, (I) Short-eared owl, (J) Boreal owl
Small: (K) Burrowing owl, (L) Northern saw-whet owl, (M,N) Eastern and Western screech owls,
(O) Flammulated owl, (P) Northern pygmy owl, (Q) Ferruginous pygmy owl, (R) Elf owl

Barn Owl

Flammulated Owl

Long-eared Owl

Northern Hawk Owl

Snowy Owl

Great Horned Owl

Elf Owl

Ferruginous Pygmy Owl

Northern Pygmy Owl

APPEARANCE: medium-size owl; long, close-set ear tufts; nicknamed "cat owl"
HABITAT: forests and forest clearings, especially coniferous woodlands and plantations
VOICE: low pitched hoot. (One writer suggests it sounds like blowing over the top of a bottle.)
FOOD: voles, mice, and a few birds, caught at night
NEST: stick nest taken over from crows; eggs 3-8, usually 4-5

Long-eared Owl *Asio otus*

APPEARANCE: small, dark-eyed owl, tiny ear tufts
HABITAT: forests of western mountains, especially ponderosa pine; migrates south in winter
VOICE: single or paired hoots that sound hollow
FOOD: beetles, moths, caterpillars, other insects, spiders, scorpions, centipedes, and millipedes
NEST: in tree cavities; eggs 2-3

Flammulated Owl *Otus flammeolus*

APPEARANCE: medium-size owl, dark eyes, pale feathers
HABITAT: towns, cities, and open areas such as prairies, farmlands, marshlands, and deserts
VOICE: raspy, gargling screeches; snores; and hisses
FOOD: mostly rodents (rats and mice), caught at night
NEST: in dark cavities in cliffs, banks, and trees, also buildings; eggs 3-7

Barn Owl *Tyto alba*

APPEARANCE: large, tall owl with ear tufts, yellow eyes; nicknamed "winged tiger" for its fierce hunting skills
HABITAT: widespread, including cities
VOICE: a series of three to eight loud, deep hoots
FOOD: mice, rabbits, birds, other owls, even skunks. Phew! Owls cannot smell well.
NEST: in trees, caves, or even on ground; takes over abandoned hawk or magpie nests; eggs 1-6, normally 2-3

Great Horned Owl *Bubo virginianus*

APPEARANCE: males mostly white, females white with dark barring
HABITAT: treeless arctic tundra, salt marshes, and sandy beaches
VOICE: usually silent, but can croak, boom, growl, or cackle
FOOD: mostly lemmings; also mice, hares, and birds
NEST: on the ground; eggs 4-9, even up to 14 when lemmings are plentiful

Snowy Owl *Nyctea scandiaca*

APPEARANCE: hawk-like, long-tailed, low and swift in flight
HABITAT: forests, forest clearings, and swamps
VOICE: hawk-like "kee-kee-kee-kee"
FOOD: voles, mice, chipmunks, and rabbits
NEST: in broken tops of snags or stumps or in tree cavities; eggs 3-7, normally 5-6

Northern Hawk Owl *Surnia ulula*

APPEARANCE: house sparrow-size owl, long tail, black nape spots that look like eyes
HABITAT: dense woodlands in foothills and mountains
VOICE: series of even, whistled hoots
FOOD: mice, large insects, small to medium-size birds
NEST: in tree cavities, often old woodpecker holes; eggs 2-7, usually 2-4

Northern Pygmy Owl *Glaucidium gnoma*

APPEARANCE: small; eye-like marks on the back of its head that may frighten **predators** (animals that hunt it for food)
HABITAT: saguaro deserts and riverbank woodlands
VOICE: long series of whistled, breathy notes
FOOD: small mammals, birds, and insects, often caught by day
NEST: in tree cavities or snags; eggs 3-5

Ferruginous Pygmy Owl *Glaucidium brasilianum*

APPEARANCE: tiny, short-tailed
HABITAT: Sonoran Desert and nearby streamside areas
VOICE: many calls, including a puppy-like bark
FOOD: mostly insects, with some scorpions and spiders; often hovers to hunt
NEST: in old woodpecker holes in cottonwoods or saguaro cactus. (The thick cactus wall insulates the elf owlets from daytime heat and cold nights.) eggs 2-4

Elf Owl *Micrathene whitneyi*

Western Screech Owl

Burrowing Owl

Spotted Owl

Eastern Screech Owl

Great Gray

Barred Owl

Northern Saw-whet Owl

Boreal Owl

Short-eared Owl

Spotted Owl — *Strix occidentalis*

APPEARANCE: medium-size; brown-eyed; whitish spots on head, back, and belly
HABITAT: old growth forests or thickly wooded canyons
VOICE: three or four bark-like hoots
FOOD: flying squirrels, wood rats, rabbits, and a few birds
NEST: in cavities in old growth trees or on stick platform nests built by squirrels, hawks, or wood rats; eggs 2-4, usually 2

Burrowing Owl — *Athene cunicularia*

APPEARANCE: robin-size owl, speckled brown, long-legged
HABITAT: short-grass or grazed grasslands; often found in prairie dog towns
VOICE: many different calls, including rattlesnake-like hiss
FOOD: insects, small mammals, and some birds
NEST: in underground burrows, usually ground squirrel or prairie dog holes, although burrowing owls can dig, too; eggs 6-11, usually 7-9

Western Screech Owl — *Otus kennicottii*

APPEARANCE: small, gray or grayish-brown, ear tufts, yellow eyes (like Eastern screech owl)
HABITAT: open woodlands, streamsides, parks, deserts
VOICE: series of short whistles that speed up
FOOD: small rodents, birds, bats, insects
NEST: in tree cavities; eggs 3-8, normally 4-5

Whiskered Screech Owl, *Otus trichopsis*
APPEARANCE, FOOD, and NEST: similar to Western screech owl **HABITAT:** oak-conifer woodlands **VOICE:** short, evenly spaced whistles

Barred Owl — *Strix varia*

APPEARANCE: medium-size; chunky, small talons
HABITAT: swampy woodlands and forests
VOICE: nine-hoot "who cooks for you, who cooks for you all," screams, chuckles, and down-slurred, quavering "oo-ahh"
FOOD: frogs, crayfish, small mammals and birds, including screech owls
NEST: in tree cavities or old hawk, crow, or squirrel nests; eggs 2-4

Great Gray Owl — *Strix nebulosa*

APPEARANCE: largest-looking owl in North America; puffed and fluffy feathers cover its relatively small, lightweight body
HABITAT: northern spruce-fir forests
VOICE: soft, mellow hooting heard up to half a mile away
FOOD: small rodents, especially voles, and some small birds
NEST: takes over stick nests built by crows or hawks; eggs usually 2-4

Eastern Screech Owl — *Otus asio*

APPEARANCE: small, grayish-brown or reddish brown, ear tufts, yellow eyes (like Western screech owl). The two colors are called color forms. An owl cannot change between colors. It is born either gray or brown.
HABITAT: forests, swamps, parks, gardens, woodlots, orchards
VOICE: gentle, horse-like whinny or long, single trill
FOOD: small rodents, birds, bats, insects
NEST: in tree cavities; eggs 3-8, normally 4-5

Short-eared Owl — *Asio flammeus*

APPEARANCE: medium-size; tawny-colored; long wings and wavering flight pattern
HABITAT: tundra, marshes, dunes, grasslands, farm fields, and other open areas
VOICE: "chu-chu-chu" sounds, barks, and squeals; male claps wings together during courtship flights to make sound **FOOD:** small rodents, caught by day. When mice are plentiful, many short-eared owls may hunt together. **NEST:** on the ground in a cup of flattened grasses; eggs usually 4-7

Boreal Owl — *Aegolius funereus*

APPEARANCE: small; chocolate-colored underparts
HABITAT: spruce-fir forests, especially near forest openings, or **deciduous** woodlands (woodlands of trees that lose their leaves in winter)
VOICE: a trill that stays on the same note
FOOD: voles, mice, shrews, and a few birds
NEST: in holes made by woodpeckers, or natural tree cavities; eggs usually 4-6

Northern Saw-whet Owl — *Aegolius acadicus*

APPEARANCE: tiny; large head appears top-heavy; yellow eyes
HABITAT: forests and woodlands, especially mountain spruce-fir forests
VOICE: long series of one-pitch notes (like a damped-down bell). The name "saw-whet" comes from raspy call that sounds like a saw being sharpened. (Whet means sharpen.)
FOOD: woodland mice, voles, shrews, and bog lemmings
NEST: in old woodpecker holes; eggs 4-7

Why Owl Has Big Eyes

ong ago, the Maker was still creating the birds and animals as they wished to be. White Owl wished he could have a long, elegant neck like Swan. White Owl wanted long, graceful legs like Heron. Owl coveted a spear-like bill. He craved brightly colored feathers. He wanted. . . . Greedy, he wanted everything other birds had.

The Maker was walking through the forest, asking each furry or feathery creature its choice. He came to Rabbit.

"If I had long legs, like the deer, I could run swiftly from bush to bush," said Rabbit. "I would like long ears, too, and a warm coat to keep out the chill winds . . . and claws like the lynx."

"Very well," said the Maker, "but all other creatures, turn away. Close your eyes. No one may watch me at my work."

Owl looked down from a perch in the tree above. "Long legs. Long legs," he kept hooting. "Long neck, long beak, lovely feathers. Quick, quick, quick."

"Shush! Close your eyes," said the Maker. "You must not watch." And he began to stretch Rabbit's ears until they were long and so thin you could almost see through them. Then he pulled on Rabbit's back legs until. . . .

Owl winked open one eye. He blinked open the other eye. Owl turned his head until he could see back over his left shoulder. He must not look. He should not look. He could not resist. And when he saw Rabbit's ears, he hooted in astonishment.

When the Maker saw that White Owl was peeking, he was very angry. He grabbed Owl from the tree and rammed Owl's head down into his shoulders. He glared at Owl until Owl's eyes grew enormous with fright. They were so enormous, they could no longer move in their sockets.

"That is all you will get," said the Maker. "Learn to live with your short neck and staring eyes. And do not look upon the day again." The Maker put Owl into a hollow tree and turned to finish his work on Rabbit. But Rabbit, scared by the angry voices, had scuttled away into the long grasses. He hopped, loppity-lop. His stretched hind legs overtook his short front feet every step of the way.

So it is to this day! Rabbits lollop along, listening for owls with their long ears. And stubby, staring owls live in the darkness, hunting rabbits, who are the cause of their exile to the night.

Retold from a folk tale of the Seneca Indians, one of the Five Nations of the Iroquois, who lived in what is now New York State

Activity: **Owls from the Inside Out**

Although some owls are active by day, most owls are nocturnal (nighttime) predators – they work the night shift. Owls have excellent eyesight, both day and night. They have acute hearing, especially for high-pitched sounds such as squeaking mice or rustling leaves. They fly on silent wings, then plunge into the darkness to capture and kill their prey. Owls are superb hunters. They have the right tools for the task.

Explore a great horned owl from the inside out and find details of its remarkable tools.

The game includes:
• an owl skeleton on page 18
• pictures of the muscles of an owl and the outside of an owl on page 19
• information on pages 18 and 21 to go with each layer of the owl you will build

You need:
• scissors
• glue or paste or an envelope

To play:
• Remove page 19 from the book and cut out the owl muscle layer and the whole owl layer. Cut along the dotted lines. Be sure to leave the tab on your owl. This will form a hinge.
• Paste the back side of the tab of the muscle layer (1). Paste it into place on top of the skeletal owl tab (rectangular dashed box).
• Paste the back side of the tab of the whole owl layer (2). Paste it in position atop the muscle layer tab. You will be able to open your owl layer by layer and view the layers underneath.
• Look for letters on the skeleton, the muscle layer, and the whole owl. The letters match letters of the text, which describes features that help the owl be a hunter.

Skeleton Layer

Paste (1) muscle layer tab and (2) whole owl tab here

A. Bony rings protect huge eyes. Owl eyes are as large as human eyes! If your eyes were as large, proportional to your head size, they would be as large as grapefruits.

B. Large, crescent-shaped ear holes lie at each side of the skull.

C. An owl's curved beak is used for shredding large prey. An owl swallows small prey whole. It has no teeth for chewing (see page 29).

D. An owl's big eyes cannot move much in the eye sockets. Imagine them like car headlights, shining forward until the car turns. The owl has a flexible neck and turns its whole head to see sideways and behind.

E. Bones are hollow and lightweight for flight. Some bones contain air sacs. They help with breathing during flight. They help the bird lose heat when it gets too hot. Owls do not sweat.

F. Four toes with long, pointed talons spread wide to catch prey.

2.

Paste back of tab – position on top of muscle layer tab (1) on page 18.

1.

Paste back of tab – position within the rectangle above skeleton on page 18.

19

Owls groom their feathers to keep them in good repair for flight and insulation. They use their beaks and claws to smooth and tidy feathers and waterproof them with oil from a special oil gland. Owls **molt** (lose old feathers and grow new ones) each year. The owl molts feathers gradually, one by one, so it can always fly.

Soft body feathers help muffle sound. If an owl were noisy, prey animals would hear it coming. The noise of the owl's own movements would prevent it from hearing prey sounds.

Many owls have one ear higher than the other. Squeaks or rustles from prey reach one of the owl's ears a fraction of a second before the other one. The owl moves its head to judge the sounds and pinpoint its prey – think of it as 3-D sound!

Muscle Layer

G. Owls focus on prey with **binocular** (two-eyed) vision. Each eye sees an object from a different angle, but the views overlap. This way of seeing helps the owl judge distance. Owls bob and turn their heads to change their viewpoint. It makes near objects stand out from the background.

Light comes into the eye through the **pupil**, the round center of the eye. At night, the pupil opens wide to let in maximum light. By day, it shuts to a pinpoint to let in only a little of the bright light. The owl "sees" when light falls on special cells at the back of the eye. These cells cause nerve messages to travel to the brain. The special cells are **rods** and **cones**. Rods work in low light and "see" in black-and-white. Owls have many rod cells. Cones work in daylight and see in color. Owls have only a few of them.

H. Powerful flight muscles attach to the breastbone.

I. Muscles and **tendons** (connections between muscle and bone) of the legs and feet close the talons to catch prey. They also clamp talons around a perch so the owl does not fall off the tree branch when it sleeps.

The Whole Owl

J. Ear tufts are just feathers. They have nothing to do with hearing. Owls may recognize other owls of their own species by the shape of their ear tufts.

K. Feathers around the eyes form saucer-shaped **facial disks**. The disks collect sounds and funnel them to the hearing ears that are beneath the feathers of the facial disks.

L. Owls close their eyes as we do. They drop their upper eyelids to meet the lower lids. Beneath these lids, owls have see-through eyelids that flick across the eyeballs to clean them and protect them when the owl is catching prey.

M. Bristly feathers around an owl's beak act as sensors. They work like a cat's whiskers.

N. Flight feathers have soft, fringed edges. The owl, with its lightweight body and large-area wings, flies using a slow wing beat. These features make flight quiet. Soft body feathers help muffle sound. If an owl were noisy, prey animals would hear it coming. The noise of the owl's own movements would prevent it from hearing prey sounds.

22

Activity: **Owls by Day**

During the day, nocturnal owls **roost** (rest). Some owls roost in caves, rock crevices, holes in banks, or in old buildings or other structures. Some roost in holes in trees. Others roost on tree branches or in low, shrubby tangles.

See if you can find 11 roosting owls in this scene.

The game includes:
• the "Owls in Hiding" picture on pages 22 and 23
• the "Owls in Hiding" key on page 24

You need:
• crayons or colored pencils

To play:
• Look for 11 hiding owls. Color them and the rest of the forest.

23

1. In most owl species, male and female owls are alike in color. (They may vary in size – the female is larger.) Most owls are brown; brownish gray; or gray with spots, speckles, or bands of light and dark colors on their feathers. This coloration is good **camouflage**. It helps owls blend with the surroundings. An owl often roosts against a tree trunk and looks like part of the tree.

2. Sometimes an owl's body posture helps hide it. Long-eared owls disguise their owlness by stretching tall and thin, with their ear tufts upright. Their slit-eyes scarcely show. Look closely in the wild! That "broken branch" could be an owl.

3. Open eyes sometimes give away an owl's position, especially if they are large, gleaming yellow eyes.

4. Some owls have eye-like markings on the back of their necks. Scientists think this pattern may deceive would-be predators into thinking the owl is watching them.

5. When an owl is threatened at its roost or nest, it half-raises its wings and puffs up its body feathers. The owl makes itself look large and opens its eyes wide. It may hiss or clack its beak in self-defense.

All these features protect owls from predators. Not many predators catch adult owls. Small owls may be eaten by larger owls, such as great horned owls. Young owls, especially in the nest, may become the prey of eagles, hawks, opossums, or raccoons.

Unlike this puzzle, you would never find eleven different roosting owls so close together in nature! Predators are spread out in nature, because each needs a large hunting area to catch enough prey.

Owls by Day

Owl-eyed butterfly

Owl or Butterfly?

Owl eyes can scare enemies. Some butterflies have evolved patterns that look like owl eyes as a way of startling their attackers. This disguise gives the butterfly a precious few seconds to escape. What if the predator does strike the butterfly? The fake eyes lie in a part of the body where the injury does least harm.

Owls by Day

Looking for real owls in the wild is a bit like doing a hidden picture puzzle. Some clues help in the search.

• *Mobbing.* Look for crows, magpies, and small songbirds flying around, squawking or twittering noisily. They may have found a roosting owl. The birds **mob** the owl, flying at it but keeping out of reach. They harass the owl until it moves to a different roost.

• *Whitewash.* Look for white, chalky droppings, or **whitewash**, in heaps on a tree branch or splattered around on branches. Whitewash often marks a well-used roost. Look in conifers in woodlands; in large, isolated cottonwoods or willows near grasslands; and in groves of trees around farms or in city parks. Whitewash on cliffs may be from an owl roost or a hawk or eagle roost or nest.

• *Pellets.* **Pellets** are compressed, undigested parts of prey that an owl coughs up. Look for pellets under trees marked with whitewash. Fresh pellets are compact, shiny, and moist. Older pellets weather and fade. They fall apart easily and bones are readily visible. (See pages 29 to 31 for more about owl pellets.)

• *Hole watching.* Look at holes in trees, especially old woodpecker holes. You may be lucky and see an owl looking back at you.

Owls on the Prowl

Ears, eyes, beaks, and talons explain how owls find and catch prey. But there are other sides to hunting besides the tools.

When do owls hunt? Where do owls hunt? How do they hunt? What do owls catch, and why?

These questions have no single answer. Each species of owl is different. Each has a time and place for hunting. Each species hunts certain prey. Each has its own **niche**. (Scientists use this special word, niche, to describe the "job" and "place" of an animal in its habitat.) Because each owl has its own niche, there is less **competition** between species.

About Niche

A new shopping center with 10 stores opens in your neighborhood. Ten store owners want to make their living selling stuff. All 10 stores are open during the same hours and sell hamburgers and nothing else. Do you think they will all stay in business? Probably not! They are in competition with each other.

Imagine instead different stores selling candy, videos, books, pets, flowers, ice cream, pizza, and toys. Add a hamburger stand open all day and another one open at night. The ten shop owners no longer compete for the same customers. With luck, they will all make a living.

The same idea applies in nature. Owls (and all predators) survive ("make a living") only if they find enough food ("customers to eat!"). It would not work to have ten owls hunting at the same time for the same food. Most would starve. Suppose some owls hunt by night, some by day. Suppose some hunt large rabbits, some hunt mice, and some hunt insects. Suppose some hunt in forests, and some in fields. Each species has its niche and avoids competition. Each owl has a better chance of surviving.

When do owls hunt?

• Many owls, such as barn owls, hunt at night. The niche of a barn owl is "nocturnal hunter of rats and mice."
• Other owls, such as pygmy owls, hunt at dusk and dawn, catching small birds as they roost. The niche of a pygmy owl is "dusk and dawn hunter of small birds and mammals."
• Great gray owls, and other owls of the far north, must hunt by daylight in summer because it never gets dark.
• Even nocturnal owls will hunt by day, when they are feeding many hungry owlets.

Where do owls hunt and how?

• Owls hunt almost everywhere – even over garbage dumps, airports, golf courses, and people's backyards.
• Some owls fly low over their hunting grounds, watching and listening.
• Some owls hunt from a favorite lookout perch, quietly watching and waiting.

What do owls catch and why?

• Vegetables? Forget it! Owls are meat-eaters. They feed on animals that feed on other animals or plants.
• Large owls tend to hunt large prey. Great horned owls eat practically anything meaty they can catch, from rabbits and skunks to insects and other owls. They usually catch what is plentiful and what gives them a decent-sized meal in return for the energy spent catching it.
• Some owls hunt small prey, such as insects, spiders, and scorpions. Other small but fierce owls catch birds, reptiles, and mammals almost as large as themselves.

Pellet Detective

An owl tears large prey with its beak. It swallows small prey whole – skulls, bones, claws, feathers, fur, and all! But an owl cannot digest the claws, bones, and fur. The stuff it can't digest is formed into a sausage-shaped pellet that takes about 8 hours to form after a meal. The owl **regurgitates**, or coughs up, the pellet through its mouth. Owls regurgitate one or two pellets every 24 hours.

Pellets can provide many clues about what owls eat. But pellets cannot tell everything about the owl's diet. After all, tender bits of meat leave no undigested remains. Scientists study pellets to learn about what owls eat. They note where the pellets were found. Bones sorted from the pellets tell the scientists what animals the owl ate. The results can be surprising. Sometimes the bones prove to be from small animals unknown before from that habitat.

Be a pellet detective on real pellets

Search for owl pellets beneath owl roosts. (Read more about this on page 26 in "Owls by Day.") Pellets are safe to handle, but always remember to wash your hands with soap after handling *ANY* animal material. Pick the dry pellets apart using forceps or toothpicks. Or soak the pellets in a margarine tub of water to which you add a drop of dishwashing liquid. Shake the tub every few minutes. The fur and bones gradually separate. Pick out the bones and spread them on a paper towel to dry.

Activity: **Be a Pellet Detective**

The objective:
• Use your detective skills to decide the least number of animals the owl must have eaten to produce each pellet.

HINT: Pellets often contain skulls, jawbones, or bird claws. They are the best clues to the number of eaten animals. The pellets also contain many small bones, such as ribs, legs, and shoulder blades. You would not expect to find all the bones from every eaten animal. Some bones break when the owl eats its prey.

The game includes:
• Bones Key on page 31 that illustrates remnants you might find in an owl pellet
• two "fake pellets" – containing drawings of bones and other undigested remains on page 31

To play:
• Imagine the drawings on page 31 represent bones found in two pellets.
• Look at the bones and compare them with the Bones Key on page 31.
• Are there more bones in each "fake pellet" than could have come from one animal? What do you think?

Pellets: Life size

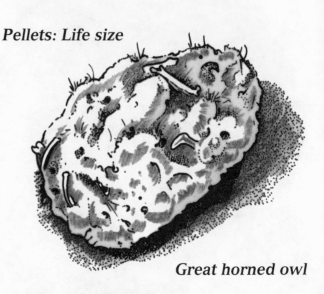

Great horned owl

Barn owl

Swainson's hawk

Not all pellets come from owls. Hawks, crows, wading birds, gulls, and even songbirds produce pellets. The pellets may contain shell fragments from insects or indigestible seeds. They usually break apart more easily than owl pellets.

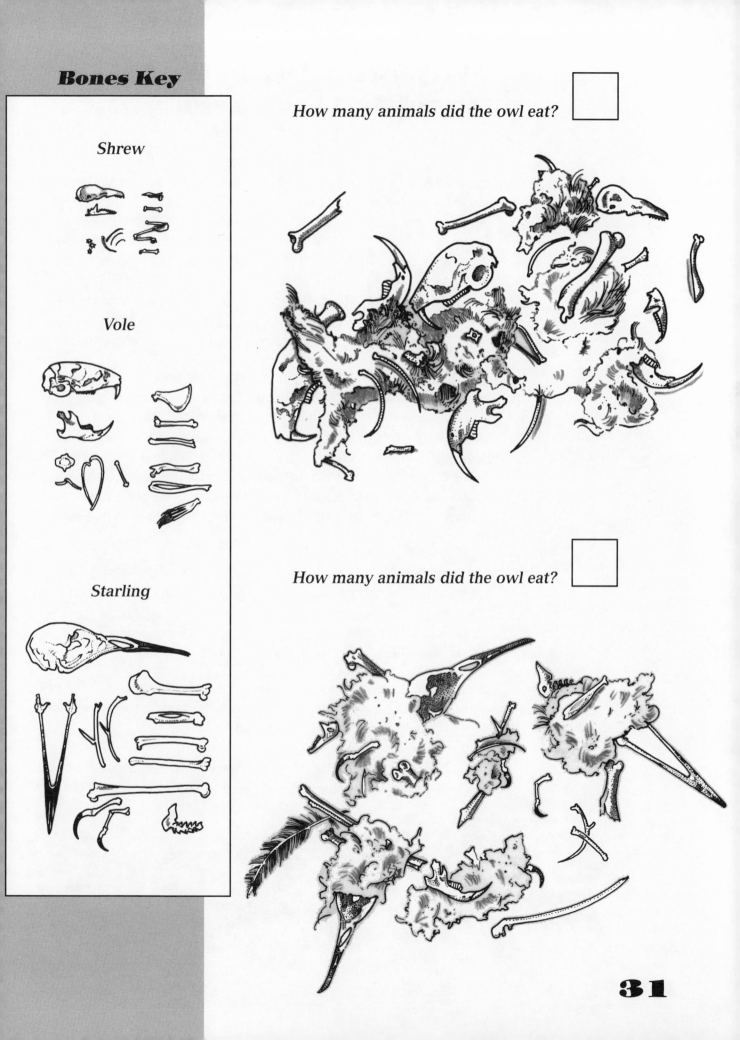

Bones Key

Shrew

Vole

Starling

How many animals did the owl eat?

How many animals did the owl eat?

31

Why Burrowing Owl Has Speckled Feathers

Long ago, beyond the great mesa called Middle Mountain, lay Prairie Dog Land. Sky holes and door mounds of prairie dogs' underground homes dotted the landscape. Grandfather Burrowing Owl and his family lived on the tallest mound in the center of the village. The owls lived peacefully with the prairie dogs. The prairie dogs respected the owls for their great dignity and wisdom and never disturbed the owls' meetings or ceremonies.

One early morning, Grandfather Burrowing Owl was teaching his family to dance. Some owls whistled and clacked their beaks in perfect rhythm, making music. Others danced, each with a bowl of yucca-plant foam* balanced atop its head. The owls stretched their wings. They bobbed and bowed. They hop-stepped back and forth on their long, spindly legs, never missing a beat. And although the steps looked clumsy, not one owl – not even the youngest among them – spilled a single drop of foam onto its sleek, brown feathers.

That morning, Coyote was prowling the byways of the village, hunting for breakfast. He heard click-clacking music and the shrill, piping song of the owls:

> *I yami hota utcha tchapikya*
> *Tokos! Tokos! Tokos! Tokos!*

Now, unlike the prairie dogs, Coyote was always sticking his nose into other animals' affairs. When he saw the owls dancing their foam dance, he was curious. He just had to stop and watch.

"Ho! Ho! Ho! Hah! Hah! Hah!" he laughed rudely. "What a silly dance. You look as if you were limping, and your legs go every-which-way."

"My friend, we dance for our own pleasure and for the good of the town," Grandfather Burrowing Owl replied. "This is a sacred performance. The limp is part of our tradition."

"Dust and devils," said Coyote, "whatever next? All the same, your music sets my feet a-tapping. I bet I can dance better than any of you. Give me a bowl of foam. I'll show you how to dance this dance."

"Your legs are too straight to do our dance," said Grandfather Burrowing Owl. He was annoyed with Coyote's boastful ways. "Take the bowl. Then break your hind legs to make them crooked so you can match our steps."

Coyote hated to be outdone. So he hit his legs with a rock to break them.

"Ow! Ow! Oh! Oh!" Coyote yowled. He put the bowl of yucca foam on his head and hobbled over to join the line of dancers.

"I'm ready – on with the music," Coyote howled. He limped and lurched from step to step. He waved his front paws wildly to keep his balance. But Coyote could not dance like the owls. The yucca foam from his bowl splashed everywhere.

"Tck! Tck! Tck!" laughed the owls, especially the young ones, who knew how hard it was to learn the owl dance. The owls laughed so hard their bowls began to spill, too. Soon the air was full of flecks of foam. They splattered Grandfather Burrowing Owl, the dancers, and the musicians like a winter blizzard, mottling their sleek, brown feathers.

That is why burrowing owls have speckled plumage, as you can see for yourself when you watch them hip-hop their comical dance.

Retold from a Zuni Indian folk tale
* The roots of the yucca plant make suds in water, like soap.

Underground Owl

Adult prairie dogs are much larger than burrowing owls. The owls eat an occasional young prairie dog, but usually they go for smaller prey.

Sometimes a whole family roosts in a row. When startled, they bob up and down like a comical chorus line doing a strange dance.

Burrowing owls have long legs, great for running around catching insects.

L ong ago, the short-grass prairie stretched for mile upon mile. Bison roamed freely across the unfenced landscape. Prairie dog towns were enormous, full of thousands of prairie dogs and hundreds of owls – just like Prairie Dog Land in the story. Imagine you are there. . . . Was Coyote up before you? Look around the prairie dog village. See who Coyote met and what he saw on his travels.

Watch out mice, voles, and insects. Burrowing owls may catch you for dinner.

Owls may roost on mounds of earth around the burrow entrances. They watch for danger. If they see something strange, they twist, turn, and bob their heads to get a better look.

When threatened, a burrowing owl may puff itself up to look larger, spread its wings, and clack its beak. Or it may duck into its hole to escape danger.

Young burrowing owls make buzzing sounds, like a rattlesnake's rattle. This sound may scare away predators. It also fools people into thinking owls and rattlesnakes share the same burrows, which is not true.

The burrowing owl nest is underground in a prairie dog hole. Burrowing owl eggs are round and white.

Rattlesnakes may live, hunt, and escape the too-hot sun in prairie dog holes.

35

News Flash!

Burrowing Owls Invade Campus

Cape Coral, Florida

In some places, burrowing owls take over gopher holes, or even dig their own burrows. At Diplomat Elementary School, burrowing owls "took over" the school campus. They built three nests in 1993 – one in the middle of the softball field! Students at the school enjoy learning about their owl neighbors. But they worry when the rains come. The school is on flat land. Heavy rains can flood the underground nests. If this happens before the owlets fledge, the nestlings drown.

When the school was built, much habitat was lost. Wildlife is limited, so the school owls and other owls in the area are really special. Someone wanted to get rid of the owls on a nearby football field. They said the owls' diggings made a mess. Students wrote letters to their local paper and town officials, asking to save the owls. It worked!

Kids Help Owls!

Boulder, Colorado

Burrowing owls need help in Boulder County. Housing developments have taken over much prairie dog habitat. Owls suffer from loss of undisturbed space.

Students from University Hill Elementary School did a survey to find out what people knew about burrowing owls. The results of the survey shocked them. Many adults did not know that letting dogs run loose through prairie dog towns harmed owls. The students began to teach family and friends about helping owls. They also designed owl note cards and sold them to raise money. Their money helped support a ten-year-old burrowing owl, C.C., or Crazy Critter, that lives in captivity. The owl cannot be released. It is too accustomed to humans and would not survive.

Sorting Owls

Many people keep their stuff tidy and easy to find by sorting it. Maybe they have a place for puzzles, a place for books, a place for pencils and crayons, and so on.

Scientists keep track of living things and the facts known about them in much the same way. They group living things by features they have in common. They start with broad groups, such as animal or plant. They divide each broad group into smaller and more specialized units. They divide groups again and again, until they have a unit that is a single species of living thing. A species has its own unique two-part scientific name. A scientific name is more exact than a common name, such as owl or hoot owl, which might describe several different birds.

KINGDOM

PHYLUM

CLASS

ORDER
Strigiformes (All owls)

Owls fit the scientific classification system like this: they belong in the KINGDOM Animalia (animals), the PHYLUM Chordata (animals with backbones), the CLASS Aves (birds), the ORDER Strigiformes (all owls). After this, owls are split into two groups, the barn owls (FAMILY Tytonidae) and the typical owls (FAMILY Strigidae). ("Typical"owl is a name given to the group, not a description. It does not mean that all owls in this group are average, standard, or alike.)

FAMILY **Tytonidae**
Barn Owls

FAMILY **Strigidae**
Typical Owls

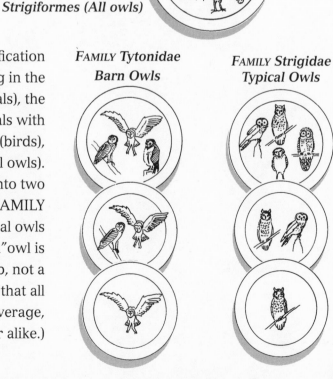

Activity: **Owl Puzzler**

Hints

Barn owls

legs: long, with bare feet

eyes: small, dark

facial disks: heart shaped

ear tufts: none

beak: long and narrow

The game includes:
• outlines on page 38 and 41 of a common barn owl (FAMILY: Barn owl) and a long-eared owl (FAMILY: Typical owl)
• puzzle pieces on page 39

You need:
• scissors
• glue or paste or an envelope

To play:
• Remove page 39, containing puzzle pieces, from your book.
• Cut out the puzzle pieces.
• Use the hints to help you sort the puzzle pieces and complete the puzzles. Watch out for extra mystery pieces to fit the "?".
• When you have completed the puzzles, you may paste the pieces in your book permanently or store them in an envelope so you can do the puzzle again.

Common Barn owl *Tyto alba*, FAMILY TYTONIDAE Barn owls

Hunts at night, over open areas. Catches rats and mice. Roosts and nests in caves, tree cavities, bank holes, barns, and buildings.

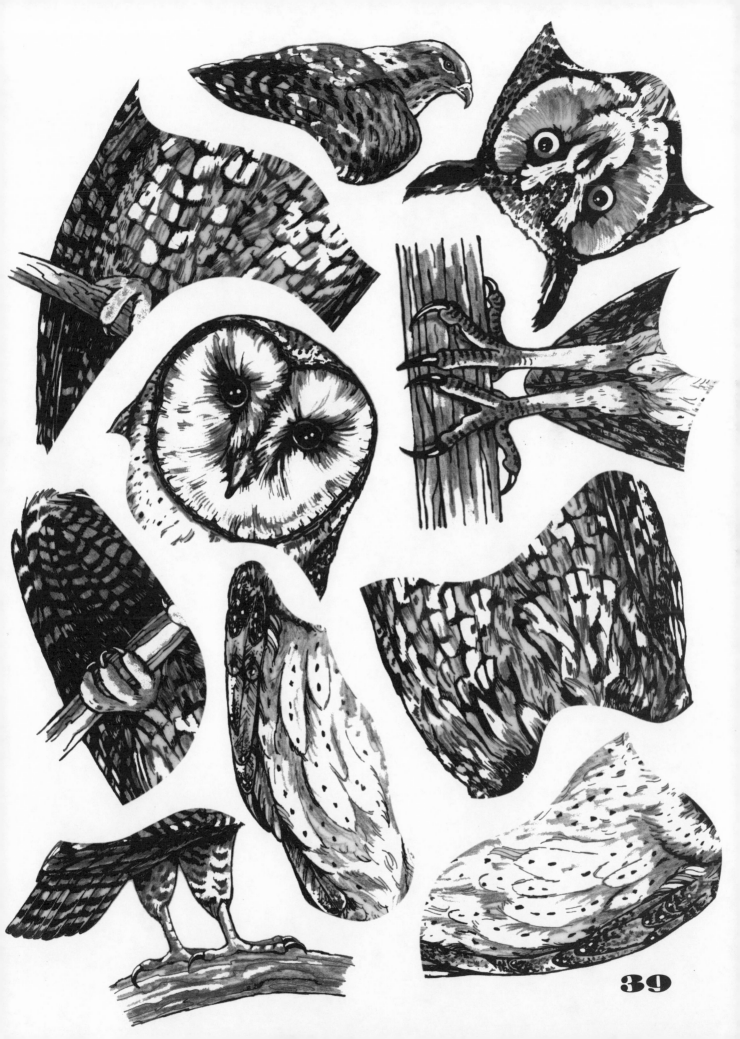

39

Long-eared owl *Asio otus*,
FAMILY STRIGIDAE Typical owls

Hunts mostly at night, in dense to open woodland. Catches voles. Nests and roosts in trees (sometimes in groups of long-eared owls in winter).

Hawks and eagles are not related to owls. The two groups have evolved some similar features because they are all birds of prey. They all lead similar lives, catching other animals for food. Hawks and eagles come before owls in most bird field guides. Owls come later, just before nighthawks. This is because scientists think owls are more closely related to nighthawks and whip-poor-wills than they are to hawks and eagles.

?

Hints

Typical owls

legs: usually quite short

eyes: large, often yellow

facial disks: rounded

ear tufts: sometimes present

beak: quite short

Rat Trap Owl

Common barn owls, or "rat trap owls," eat rats, mice, voles, shrews, and other small rodents that would otherwise damage farmers' crops. Only on rainy nights, when mice run silently on wet leaves, might the owl fail to catch enough prey. One scientist figured that a single owl catches about 2,000 rodents a year. That is 5 or 6 rodents a night. Owls are valuable to have around the farm.

Farms used to have many small fields separated by hedgerows – good owl hunting habitat. Often, there were cliffs, banks, or hollow trees in which owls could nest. Even if natural nest sites were few, most farms had owl-friendly barns. Farmers built the barns with "owl boards." These owl doorways let barn owls roost and nest in the barn. The owl boards were an "open invitation" to the owls that they were welcome.

Nowadays, new barns are built differently. They are not so owl-friendly. Farms have huge open fields with few tall nesting trees. Many farmers use pesticides to control unwanted plants or animals.

Loss of nesting space, loss of hunting habitat, and loss of prey by poisoning all harm barn owls. Luckily, some farmers are putting up owl boxes, to entice the rat trap owls back.

Snowy Owls of the Tundra

Snowy owls are snow white, with just a touch of brown or slate gray. Feathers almost hide their small beaks and cover their legs. These large owls blend with the snow of the tundra where they live. In summer, they stand out against tawny grasses and bright wildflowers. Unlike arctic foxes, ptarmigan, and snowshoe hares, snowy owls do not change their color from winter to summer.

Summer is short on the tundra, but daylight lasts around the clock. Plants grow fast. They provide food and cover for lemmings (the favorite prey of snowy owls), mice, and voles.

Snowy owls nest among hummocks and rocky outcrops. The nest is a scratched-out hollow on the ground. The female lays four to nine eggs, or more in years when prey is plentiful. It takes her several days. Each egg hatches about 30 days after it was laid. Both parents hunt food for their hungry brood. Owlets scatter from the nest before they can fly. If they spread out, they face less danger from arctic foxes on the hunt.

Snowy owls depend on lemmings for much of their food. Luckily for owls, lemmings raise large families. Young lemmings are soon old enough to raise large families themselves. Lemming numbers increase quickly. But every three to five years there are so many lemmings they do not have enough food. They move from the area or die. This means a food shortage for snowy owls. Many fly south in search of food – even to places as far south as Florida.

In an average winter, some snowy owls stay in their breeding grounds. Others drift south, to where food is more plentiful. These journeys are not true migrations. The owls don't set out for a certain destination and return from there the following spring. They move just far enough to find prey. Perhaps they travel to Boston's Logan Airport, like the owls in the next story, perhaps to the state in which you live?

Activity: **Origami Owl**

You need:

• scissors

• a blank piece of white paper cut in the shape of a *perfect* square

Fold this origami owl to store your owl cards. You may wish to color it to resemble a snowy owl – one like the pictures on pages 43 and 45. Or choose your favorite owl from elsewhere in the book.

Use both sides of the origami owl to hold your 18 owl trading cards.

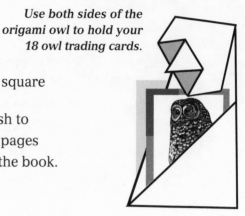

1.

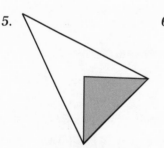

crease

Make a diagonal crease.

2.

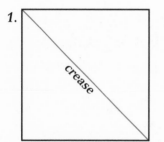

Crease along dashed lines and fold each side toward center.

3.

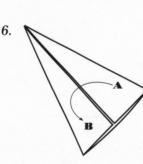

Your origami will look like this.

4.

B
A

Turn over to other side – crease along dashed line and fold A to B.

5.

Your origami will look like this.

6.

A
B

Turn over to other side – fold in half A to B.

7.

A
1
2

slip your finger between the two halves

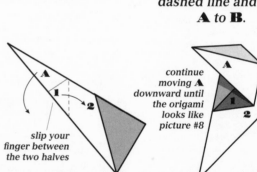

continue moving A downward until the origami looks like picture #8

A
1
2

Slip your finger between the two halves and fold A downward, creasing along the dashed lines. Area 1 will fold flat against area 2.

8.

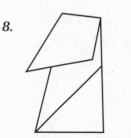

Your origami will look like this.

9.

A
B

Crease along dashed line and fold A to B.

10.

Your origami will look like this.

11.

B
A

Crease along dashed line and fold A to B.

12.

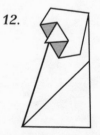

Your origami owl will look like this when it is completed.

Giving a Hoot for Owls!

Not many young people are lucky enough to work with snowy owls up close. Danielle Smith is an exception. Danielle, 13, and her brother, Joshua, 9, help their father study snowy owls at Logan Airport in Boston, Massachusetts.

Why would snowy owls spend the winter at a busy airport?

Danielle thinks the open spaces and short grass may look like tundra to the owls. The snowy owls come to Logan to find food: rats, mice, small birds, pigeons, ducks, muskrats, and skunks. "We see remains of skunks, but I've never seen a snowy owl catch a skunk. I've never held a skunky-smelling owl, but I've held a fishy-smelling owl!" Danielle said. "Once, we watched from our car while a snowy owl caught a great blue heron." (Great blue herons are large, long-legged wading birds, much bigger than snowy owls.) "The heron fought hard and poked the owl with its beak. It was a hard battle, but in the end the owl won."

Is it sad to see owls catch and kill their prey?

"Sometimes it can be sad," Danielle said, "but not really. I know that if owls don't catch their prey, they cannot survive. It's the way it has to work."

The snowy owls usually arrive at Logan Airport in November. From November to April, Danielle and her family go to the airport on weekends, taking binoculars and field guides. They watch for owls in the grassy areas between the runways. Owl numbers vary. One year there were 5 owls. Another year there were 49, 23 of them on a single day!

Danielle's father sets trap nets to capture owls and mark them. That way, Danielle, Joshua, and their father can recognize individual owls and record their behavior. Each owl gets a paint dot of a different color on the back of its head. The paint is harmless and washes off in a few months. Each bird is fitted with a numbered metal leg band, checked for health, and weighed. Danielle records this information, then sets the bird free.

What does it feel like to hold an owl?

"Cool!" Danielle said. "You have this sense of wonder that it can fly. Snowy owls are magnificent birds, not as heavy as you might think. Some hiss and clack their beaks when you hold them, but most owls are quite calm." Even so, Danielle handles each owl with care. She cradles it in her arms and holds its legs so the owl's sharp talons will not hurt her. She watches out for the owl's beak, too!

Are owls bothered by the noise of the planes?

Danielle does not think so. "We set a trap near an active runway and baited it with a starling. The owl heard the starling squawking over the noise of the airplane and swooped down!"

Danielle and Joshua study owl pellets and have found bones of rats, mice, voles, and also bird skulls in the almost 5,000 owl pellets they have collected!

Danielle has worked with snowy owls and other birds of prey for about 10 years! She sounds excited when she talks about them. One day, she hopes to be a veterinarian specializing in **ornithology** (the study of birds). Good luck, Danielle!

Owl Song

Pussy said to the Owl, "You elegant fowl,
how charmingly sweet you sing!"

– Edward Lear, *The Owl and the Pussycat*

Owls hunt alone, mostly at night. They fly silently and are seldom seen. But they give themselves away by their voices. Each species of owl has its own set of calls. (See your "Owl Cards" for the most common calls of each species.) Shrieks, puppy-like barks, hoots and hisses, whinnies and whistles – the calls may seem strange to us, but to the owls they are a way of "talking."

An owl may call for many reasons:
• A male owl calls to attract a mate and hopes a female owl will reply. It would do the male owl no good to have bright, flashy plumage to attract his mate. He does his courting in the dark. The female knows him by his voice and body shape. During the breeding season, listen for male and female owls calling back and forth – an owl duet.
• A male owl calls to defend his nesting **territory**, his place, warning off other male owls. In owl language, he is saying "keep out."
• Young owls call to beg for food.
• Owls that feel threatened clack with their beaks and tongues and hiss in self-defense.

Scientists use owl calls to find out which owls live and perhaps nest in an area. Sometimes, scientists "call in" the owls by playing tape recordings of owl calls. The researchers walk or drive chosen trails or roads. Each night, they stop at the same places to play the calls. They play calls of small owls first. Finally, they play the call of the great horned owl. (If they played the great horned owl call first, any small owls in the area would be afraid to call or come.) The scientists play each call for about two minutes. Then they listen for about two minutes. If an owl is nearby, it will call back or even fly in to investigate the sounds.

Cut along dashed line and remove semi-circle

Cut along dashed lines and remove this strip.

A

Cut along dashed lines

Cut along dashed lines and remove this strip.

A Nest of Owls

Imagine. . . a wild place not far from a city. It has ponds, cattail marshes, and a river. People made the ponds when they mined buried gravel from the flood plain of the river. They used the gravel to build roads. That was years ago. Now, the area is overgrown. A tangle of snowberry and wild currant bushes grows beneath willows and tall cottonwoods. They provide cover and a home for cottontail rabbits, skunks, foxes, raccoons, rock squirrels, and many small birds. The ponds and the farm fields nearby are great horned owl nesting territory – defended from other male great horned owls who intrude.

Follow the instructions on pages 52 and 53 to assemble your nest of great horned owls.

A Nest of Owls

Early winter. The male owl and the female owl call to one another, *who-hu-who who who*, like a question and answer. This call is their courting duet. As the male calls, his tail bobs up and his white throat patch gleams. Great horned owls pair for life. They do not build homes but take over empty hawk or magpie nests. Family life begins.

Mid-winter. The female lays her first egg and begins to **incubate** (sit on the egg to keep it warm). The egg is about the size of a jumbo chicken egg, but rounder. The

female lays one or two more eggs in the next few days. She warms the eggs with the body heat from her **brood patch**, a special area of skin with no feathers. She keeps the eggs tucked under her breast feathers. The leafless trees offer no shelter or protection. The female owl sits there, come rain, come snow, come sun. Only the top of her head and her two tufty ears show above the nest.

Thirty days later. The first owlet hatches. It is about the size of a domestic chick. Its eyes are closed and it is fuzzy, helpless, and wobbly – but hungry. The male

owl brings food. The female tears chunks of meat to feed her new owlet. The owlet eats and grows. It gets a head start on the next-to-hatch. Strong, big, and pushy, it always grabs the first food. Of the three owlets, it has the best chance of surviving, even if food is scarce.

(Over)

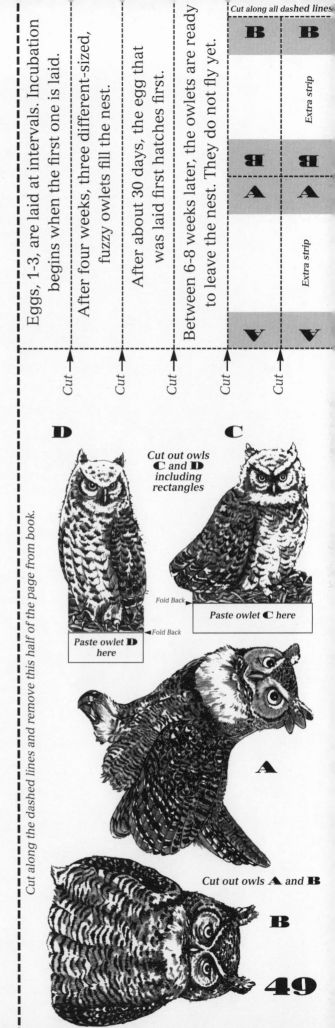

Cut along all dashed lines

Eggs, 1-3, are laid at intervals. Incubation begins when the first one is laid.

After four weeks, three different-sized, fuzzy owlets fill the nest.

After about 30 days, the egg that was laid first hatches first.

Between 6-8 weeks later, the owlets are ready to leave the nest. They do not fly yet.

Cut along the dashed lines and remove this half of the page from book.

Cut out owls **C** and **D** including rectangles

Fold Back

Paste owlet **C** here

Fold Back

Paste owlet **D** here

Cut out owls **A** and **B**

49

Caption

Caption

Caption

Caption

Four more weeks pass. The three owlets are almost as big as their parents. They are still fuzzy but are beginning to grow regular feathers. The adults take turns to hunt for food. Their young are always hungry! Owls time their nesting well. Owlets hatch when mice, voles, and rabbits are raising their families.

Two more weeks pass. The trees show a shimmer of green. The nest overflows with large, clumsy-looking owlets. The owlets flop onto branches near the nest. They cannot fly, but they climb around in the tree. Each day, they become more daring.

Ten weeks after hatching. The owlets learn to fly. They are clumsy at first – flying takes practice. Once they can fly, the owlets trail after their parents. They beg for food even when they begin to hunt for themselves. The family stays together through the summer and early fall. Great horned owls are **resident** and use the same area all year.

Winter comes again. It is time for the adult owls to breed. It is time for the young to leave and find territories of their own.

paste this gray area of strip to gray area on back of eggs picture

cut →

Cut along the dashed line.

d up →

paste owlet D here

paste owlet C here

paste caption here

Cut along the dashed line.

All owls are protected

Great horned owls sometimes prey on domestic chickens and geese, and even cats. To the owls, these animals are ordinary prey. To the people whose animals die, the owls are villains. People shot and trapped many great horned owls in the past. Even now, some owls are shot, although it is against the law. All owls are protected.

paste caption here

cut →

paste caption here

cut →

paste caption here

cut →

Cut along the dashed line.

paste picture here

51

paste "Pull Upward" strip here

B

Cut along
dashed
lines

paste this entire white area right
to the edges

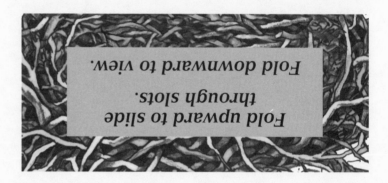

Fold upward to slide
through slots.
Fold downward to view.

Activity:
Great Horned Owl Nest

The game includes:
• the story "A Nest of Owls" on pages 48 to 50
• the four nest scenes and a "Pull Upward"
strip on page 51
• four owl portraits, four owl statements, and
mounting strips on page 49

You need:
• scissors
• glue or paste or adhesive tape

Before playing:
• Read the story "A Nest of Owls" on pages 48
to 50.

Activity: Great Horned Owl Nest

Continued from page 52

To play:

Step 1. On page 51: Cut along the dashed lines, removing the outer strip with the three nest pictures.
• Cut the "Pull Upward" strip along the dashed lines.
• Paste the "Pull Upward" strip to the back of the "eggs" scene, matching the gray areas. The "Pull Upward" arrow will show above the "eggs" scene.
• Cut the scene with one large owl along the dashed lines. Fold upward along the solid line so the picture is inside. (*Note: A portion of page 51 will remain in the book.*)

Step 2 continued:

• Weave the "**B**" strip under the slit you cut so the "**B**'s" show above the nest picture. Paste owl portrait "**B**" onto this mounting strip, matching the "**B**'s." (Use a tiny dab of paste!) You should be able to move your owl up and down!
• Bend back the tabs on owlets "**C**" and "**D**" and paste them to the matching spaces in the fold-down frame of the double frame picture. Your two owlets will stand up!

• Paste this scene to your strip. Make sure the edges are stuck.

Step 2. On page 49: Cut along the vertical dashed line, removing the outer half of the page. Cut out the four owl statements, the owl portraits, and mounting strips "**A**" and "**B**."
• Review the story and paste each caption below the picture to which it belongs.
• Cut along the dashed lines "**B**" on the back side of the "eggs" scene.

Step 3. On page 48: Cut along the dashed lines "**A**" near the tree branches. Weave the "**B**" strip through the slits. Paste owl portrait "**A**" just like you did with owl portrait "**B**." Now owl "**A**" will bob and bow.
• On page 48: Cut and remove the white strips above and below the nest. On the back side of page 48 (page 47), weave the entire picture strip through the bottom slit, then up through the top slit. *Now on page 48 you can view your nest of owls one frame at a time.*

Owl Fortunes

Northern spotted owls are in the news. You may have heard the stories and wondered why Northern spotted owls are causing so much concern.

The reason is there are far fewer Northern spotted owls than there used to be. Maybe between 2,000 and 4,000 pairs are left. They are **threatened** (at risk of becoming endangered or extinct). By law, they must be protected. But there is a problem. Spotted owls need old growth forests in which to nest and hunt. Many people want to cut old growth forests to provide wood. There is no longer enough old growth forest left to go around. You might say the Northern spotted owl's fortune is in doubt.

This game uses a "fortune teller" to explore some of the things that might happen to the Northern spotted owl.

Years ago, children in England used to make "fortune tellers" out of folded paper. They invented fortunes, like in fortune cookies, to write inside. Then they asked each other to choose a number to get to a secret fortune.

This game uses a "fortune teller" to explore some of the things that might happen to the Northern spotted owl.

Activity: Owl Fortune Teller

The game includes:
- the "fortune teller" below
- picture guides on page 57

You need:
- scissors
- crayons or colored pencils

directions continued on page 57

Cut along dashed lines.

Loggers cannot cut old growth forests without affecting owls. They can cut planted trees instead – and spare the owls. But young trees provide less wood.

Spotted owls may survive if enough of their habitat – old growth forest – is saved.

Sustainable forests produce wood every year. Planting matches cutting. The forests are never used up. These forests are best for us all in the long haul – owls, too.

Spotted owls need old growth forest. They cannot adapt quickly to another habitat.

Many living things besides owls need old growth forest. The Northern spotted owl is a symbol of the survival of them all.

We depend on wood for our building needs. If we must think of ways to use small trees – not giants – for our building, owls will not be harmed.

We use paper (made from trees) for many things: grocery sacks, tissues, books, newspapers. We can reduce, reuse, and recycle to save forests – and owls.

Newly planted seedlings are forests of the future. Even so, planting new forests may not help owls. They need mature forests now.

What is an Old Growth Forest?

An **old growth forest** is forest 200 to many hundreds of years old. It holds seedlings, mature trees, forest giants, standing dead trees, and fallen and decaying trees. It has light, sunny clearings formed where trees fall.

Old growth forests grow in layers. Grasses, wildflowers, and ferns grow at ground level. Shrubs and small trees form the **understory**, the layer that does not reach up to the light. Tall, old trees form the **canopy**, or topmost layer.

These layers make the forest rich and diverse. They provide habitat for fungi, plants, and all kinds of animals, including bugs and beetles, centipedes and salamanders, woodpeckers, squirrels, deer – and Northern spotted owls.

Activity: Owl Fortune Teller

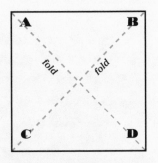

1. Fold **A** to **D**, make a triangle, crease the folded edge, open it again. Do the same matching **B** to **C**.

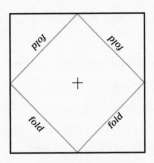

2. Fold the four points to meet at the middle "+" crease. They will cover the old growth story.

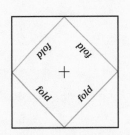

3. Turn your paper over and fold the four points of the square to meet at the middle "+" crease again.

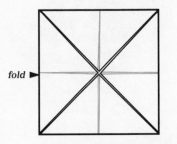

4. Keep the small square you made the same way up. Fold it in half to make a rectangle.

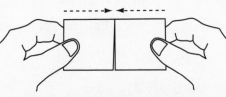

5. Pick up your folded paper by the narrow edges and move your fingers together. Your paper will have four "wings."

6. Reach underneath with your thumbs and index fingers – one in each cup. Your fortune teller is ready to play.

Continued from page 55

To play:

• Cut page 55 from your book along the dashed line.

• Cut the page along the dashed line to make a square.

• Read "What Is an Old Growth Forest?" on page 56 before you fold.

• With the pictures facing down, fold according to picture guides above.

To tell owl fortunes:

• Ask a friend to choose a number between one and nine.

• "Pump" the owl fortune teller that number of times.

• When you stop, a choice of four pictures will show. Ask your friend to choose one of them.

• Show your friend the picture that goes with the one he or she chose, then read the "fortune" underneath that flap.

Owl Fortunes

You have played "owl fortunes." Perhaps you know some of the reasons the owl has hit the headlines. You may be wondering, why bother to save the Northern spotted owl? After all, species have become extinct before. (Think of dinosaurs, dodos, saber-toothed tigers, and passenger pigeons.)

It is not only the spotted owls that would go. Owls are **indicators**, species whose presence says, "This is old growth forest in good health." Owls are symbols of a larger fight to save old growth forests and all the species that belong in them.

Shall we have owls, or forest products and jobs for people, or both? You can see from "owl fortunes" that choices are not simple or easy. There are no right or wrong answers. Owls and people share the same earth. What we do to the owls cannot be separated from what we do to habitat that sustains people, too.

Humans are not endangered. There are millions of us, and more every day. People use a lot of land for their cities, roads, and airports – land that once was habitat for plants and animals.

Can we learn to use space and the riches of the earth sparingly, so we do not survive at the expense of owls and other creatures? What do you think?

How Much Forest?

No one really knows how much old growth forest the Northern spotted owls need. Suppose owl habitat is split into separate fragments. Birds are so far apart they may not find mates, breed, and have young. Also, when few owls remain, the loss of even one becomes important. A single flood, fire, or storm in the wrong place could wipe out a whole group of owls. Scientists think a species is bound to become extinct if the number of individuals drops below a critical number. Northern spotted owl populations have not yet dropped that low.

Dead or Alive?

How long do owls live?

Owls may live many years in captivity. They are safe from life's hazards. Captive owls show how long an owl might live in the wild if it was lucky! Owls do not generally live as long in the wild. How do we know? Facts about the life span of wild owls come from banding the birds. (Read about banding snowy owls on pages 45 and 46.) If a banded owl is found dead, the band tells how long the bird lived.

An owl is most at risk in its first year of life. If it survives its first year, it may live to a reasonably old age.

Some old owls:
In the wild

Great horned owl	27 1/2 years
Common barn owl	15 1/2 years
Elf owl	5 years

Captive

European eagle owl	68 years
Great horned owl	38 years
Common barn owl	51 years

How do owls die?

Owls die of many causes. Some are eaten by predators. Some die of disease, starvation, or old age. Others are killed in accidents. They may fly into barbed wire fences or get hit by cars. Some owls are caught in traps meant to catch coyotes, foxes, or other mammals. Some are shot, although it is against the law. All owls are protected by law, because they are valued as important predators. Poisons in food-prey claim some owls' lives. An owl may eat rodents that have fed on poisons or on plants sprayed with pesticides. The poisons and pesticides concentrate in the owl's body, making it sick or even killing it.

Loss of habitat does the most harm to owls. Each newly built house, each new airport or highway, each new shopping center means a loss of owl hunting and nesting space.

Owl Prowl

Owls live all around us, in both country and city. You may not think of cities as good wildlife areas, but they can be. You need to develop a special awareness to see or hear wildlife amid the rush and noise of the city. With practice, you can "tune out" the city and "tune in" to nature. The wildlife is there!

The best advice for owl prowlers is "walk slowly, watch closely, listen carefully."

Where to look

- a city park
- a cemetery
- the edge of a woodlot
- a mountain campsite
- a tree-lined lake or riverbank
- especially, anywhere you have seen owl signs by day

What to look for

- whitewash
- pellets below a whitewashed tree or at the base of a cliff or bank hole
- By day: mobbing. Little birds may give away a roosting owl.
- By night: eyeshine. Many nighttime animals, including some owls, have a layer at the back of their eyes that reflects light. It improves their night vision. Shine a flashlight around the area where you are watching. It may pick up eyeshine, or reflected light, from the eyes of owls and other animals.

What to listen for

• Owls calling. Many libraries have tape recordings of owl calls for you to borrow. That way, you can get an idea of the calls before you go owl prowling.

When to look and listen

• September and January to March are the best months to hear owls.
• Any time in winter, look for roosting owls in leafless trees.
• Look for owls on moonlit nights, when it is dry and still. Owls like these nights best for hunting.

Event to attend

• Join a wildlife expert for calling in owls on an official "owl prowl."

PARENTS: Official owl prowls are sometimes offered by national parks, recreation departments, nature centers, local Audubon Society chapters, and other outdoor-oriented groups.

This activity is a safe and informative way to learn about owls at night.

The Last Word

In the past, many people feared owls because they did not know much about them. The owls' spine-chilling shrieks and hoots heard in the dead of night reinforced people's beliefs that owls were evil omens or spirits of the dead.

Now, people know more about owls – not only their lives but the important role they play in nature. The same calls that once frightened superstitious people now thrill owl lovers. The *who-hu-who who who* is no longer an unanswered question in the night. It is a reminder that a *Very Important Predator* is on duty in the neighborhood.

Bibliography

Burnie, David. 1988. *Eyewitness Books: Bird*. Alfred A. Knopf, New York, New York.

Coldrey, Jennifer. 1988. *The Owl in the Tree*. (Oxford Scientific Films) Animal Habitats. Gareth Stevens Publishing, Milwaukee.

Esbensen, Barbara Juster. 1991. *Tiger with Wings*. Orchard Books. Franklin Watts, Inc., New York, New York.

Hammerstrom, Frances, and Donald L. Malick. 1984. *Eagles, Hawks, Falcons, and Owls of America: A Coloring Album*. Roberts Rinehart, Inc., Niwot, Colorado, and The Raptor Education Foundation.

National Audubon Society. 1991. Video. *Owls – Up Close*. Nature Science Network, Inc., Carrboro, North Carolina.

National Geographic Society. 1983. *Field Guide to the Birds of North America*. National Geographic Society, Washington, D.C.

Sadoway, Margaret Wheeler. 1981. *Owls, Hunters of the Night*. Lerner Publications Company, Minneapolis, Minnesota.

Smith, Danielle. 1993. "Now Landing at Logan." *Ranger Rick* (February). National Wildlife Federation, Leesburg Pike, Virginia.

Yolan, Jane. 1987. *Owl Moon*. Philomel Books, New York, New York.

Zuni pottery figurine

More About Pellets

Parents: You can sterilize pellets, if you prefer. Spread the pellets on a disposable cookie tray. Heat them in a conventional oven at 300° Fahrenheit for 30 minutes. Or microwave the pellets for 7 minutes on a microwave-safe tray.

If you have no luck finding fresh pellets, you can buy pellets from:

Pellets, Inc.
P.O. Box 5484
Bellingham, Washington 98227-5484

This company also sells bone-sorting charts and a booklet, *The Barn Owl & the Pellet,* that contains skull keys.

Glossary

binocular (buh NAHK yuh luhr) – a kind of vision in which both eyes see the same scene so the animal can judge distance and speed.

brood patch (BROOD pach) – a small patch on the belly without feathers under which the eggs are kept warm.

camouflage (KAM uh flahj) – colors, shapes, or behaviors that help an animal blend with the surroundings.

canopy (KAN uh pee) – the topmost layer of a forest, containing the tallest trees that reach the light.

competition (kam puh TISH uhn) – what results when two or more animals seek to use a resource in the same place at the same time.

cone (KOHN) – a light-sensitive cell in the eye that sees color.

deciduous (dih SIHJ uh wuhs) – a tree that loses its leaves in winter.

facial disk (FAY shuhl DIHSK) – saucer-shaped disk of moveable feathers around the hidden ears of owls that direct sound to the ears.

habitat (HAB uh tat) – the place where an animal lives.

incubate (IHN kyuh bayt) – sit on eggs and hatch them by the warmth of the body.

indicator (IHN duh kayt uhr) – a species whose presence or absence gives information about the health of an ecosystem.

mob / mobbing (MAHB / MAHB ihng) – the act of small birds crowding and annoying a roosting owl.

molt (MOHLT) – to shed and replace feathers.

niche (NIHCH) – the job and place of an animal in its habitat.

nocturnal (NAHK tuhrn l) – active at night.

old growth forest (OHLD GROHTH FAWR uhst) – mature forest, older than two hundred years, containing trees in all stages of growth and a rich forest floor, understory, and canopy.

ornithology (awr nuh THAHL uh jee) – the study of birds.

owlet (OW luht) – a young owl

pellet (PEHL uht) – compressed, undigested parts of prey regurgitated through the mouth.

predator (PREHD uht uhr) – animal that hunts and kills other animals for food.

pupil (PYU puhl) – the central area of the eye through which light enters.

regurgitate (ree GUHR juh tayt) – cough up material through the mouth.

resident (REHS uh dehnt) – bird that lives in the same area all year.

rod (RAHD) – a light-sensitive cell important for seeing in low light, which sees black and white.

roost (ROOST) – to sleep, or a place where birds rest or sleep.

species (SPEE sheez) – set of animals that are grouped together for classification, because they are alike and can interbreed.

sustainable (suh STAY nuh buhl) – able to go on and on without using up a resource.

tendon (TEHN duhn) – tough, stringy connection between muscles and bones.

territory (TEHR u tohr ee) – the area an owl defends against intruders.

threatened (THREHT ehnd) – a species whose numbers are declining dangerously low, that is listed and protected by the government.

understory (UHN duhr stohr ee) – the layer of small trees in a forest that can grow in shade.

whitewash (HWEYET wawsh) – excrement, or droppings, from a bird.